HOW TO PLAN A FUNERAL AND SAVE MONEY

Gary M. Thomas MBA, CFSP, CMSP

authorHOUSE®

AuthorHouse™
1663 Liberty Drive
Bloomington, IN 47403
www.authorhouse.com
Phone: 1-800-839-8640

Published by AuthorHouse 12/30/2011

ISBN: 978-1-4685-2484-0 (sc)
ISBN: 978-1-4685-2483-3 (e)

TABLE OF CONTENTS

Passing

*We go, like flowers
into the night
blooming, in sunshine
reaching for the light.
Then fading - as the light grows dim
to allow new flowers
to begin.*

INTRODUCTION

It is never easy to accept death. After hearing that a loved one has died, we may feel angry, confused or emotionally numb. We may not know how to express our feelings of loss, or how to say good-bye to the person who has died. However, we do need to work through these feelings and that is what makes a funeral so important. A funeral is a ritual that can help focus our emotions and bring meaning to the experience of death.

"Rituals link us with the past and the future," explains Dr. Judith Stillion, a professor of psychology at Western Carolina University. "We have rituals for this most important passage of life."

The funeral serves as a means to commemorate the deceased, but just as importantly, it helps the survivors to heal emotionally. When somebody we love dies, we experience the pain of grief. Even though grief hurts, it is not something to avoid. Grief is part of the healing process that allows us to separate ourselves from the deceased person and to go on with our lives.

A funeral gives mourners ritual "permission" to express feelings of sadness and loss. Funerals also stimulate mourners to begin talking about the deceased, one of the first steps toward accepting the death. In fact, people who do not attend the funeral of a loved one because they want to deny death may suffer from unresolved grief and anger several months later.

To resolve their grief, mourners need to accept the reality of death not only on an intellectual level, but on an emotional level as well. It is for this reason that open casket visitation periods precede funerals.

Dr. Stillion said she used to feel that viewings were a barbaric custom, but her research into grief has changed her mind. "Nothing helps you accept death as much as seeing the dead person," she said, "it helps with grieving because it shows there is no return."

Funerals are the emotional element of the death that your family has to manage. You have the option of completing all of the planning process yourself including your will, estate planning etc. so they do not also have to handle these issues as well. All of these items are covered in depth in later chapters.

WHY WE HAVE FUNERALS

Alan D. Wolfelt, Ph.D., wrote the following list of reasons on the importance of the funeral ceremony in *Bereavement Magazine*:

1. Funerals provide us with a structure to support and assist mourners through their initial period of mourning. Family and friends are able to be together to gain support from each other.

2. Funerals provide a time to honor, remember, and affirm the life of the person who has died.

3. Funerals carry out the meaning of the people making use of them--the meanings that often give the mourner the sense that even in death, life goes on.

4. Funerals allow for the "search for meaning" within the context of one's individual, religious, or philosophical framework.

5. Funerals assist us in acknowledging and confirming that someone we have had a relationship with has died.

6. Funerals allow a focus for the natural expression of thoughts and feelings related to the loss.

7. Funerals allow for the recollection of memories of the person, thereby allowing for movement from a "relationship of presence" to a "relationship of memory."

8. Funerals provide an opportunity to give testimony to the value of life and living. In having a funeral, we acknowledge that the person's life has had meaning and purpose.

9. Funerals are a time to say "thank you" for having had the privilege of knowing and caring about the person who has died.

10. Funerals are a means of socially acknowledging that our life has changed-- that a significant loss has occurred that will mean our life is now different from when the person we loved was alive.

FUNERAL SERVICE OPTIONS

There are many options for you to choose from for your funeral services. In arranging for a funeral ceremony, it is important to communicate your wishes or those of the deceased to your funeral provider. The funeral provider will give advice and direction about available service options. There is no right or wrong way to plan your funeral service, any option you select must meet your wishes and desires.

Memorialization is a time-honored tradition practiced by caring people through the centuries. As survivors, we care about and want to remember those who precede us in death. Selecting and establishing a permanent memorial for a family member or a loved one not only satisfies an immediate need, but also fulfills the need to preserve our heritage. Memorials are stepping-stones to the past and to the future. They link the generations.

Many families make their memorialization selections in advance in order to eliminate the need to make decisions during a time of stress. Whether a memorialization purchase is made prior to need or at a time of need, you will want to be familiar with the many available options.

Funeral Ceremony

Your view of what suits you for a funeral ceremony will vary significantly from another loved one or even from the funeral service professional. You need to convey exactly what you want your funeral service to include:

- Do you want a service?
- Do you want a period of viewing prior to the service?
- Do you want an open or closed casket?
- Do you want to be cremated? If so, do you want a casket?
- Which cemetery do you want to use?
- Which urn do you want?
- Do you want special music?
- Do you want special flowers? (Or in lieu of flowers do you want donations)
- Do you want the ceremony at the funeral chapel or your place of worship?
- Do you want family or friends to participate in the ceremony?
- Do you have a specific person that you want to perform the ceremony?
- What charity would you like to receive financial contributions?
- Have you given your funeral service professional all contact information for the participants?

These and other decisions are for you to make. This is your opportunity to plan your funeral service exactly as you would like it. A personalized ceremony reflects the life of the deceased and has special meaning for those present. Today, arrangements are as individual as the people who make them.

Cremation

The number of people choosing cremation has increased significantly over the past several years. Contrary to common belief, cremation does not limit your choices, but actually increases them. You now have unlimited options as to the disposal of your cremated remains. They can be buried, scattered or held by a loved one.

Cremation need not replace the funeral traditions, which have become meaningful to many families. Cremation memorial assures that you can preserve the comforting values of funeral traditions, as well as provide a fitting tribute to honor a life lived. A funeral service usually takes place before the cremation process begins. It is similar to a funeral service followed by a ground burial. The means of final disposal is a personal choice, and one that should meet your needs and wishes. There is no right or wrong way when making cremation arrangements.

To assist you, the options open to you are explained here. This is not intended to be a complete list, only alternatives for your personal consideration.

Options Following Cremation:

Burial of the Cremated Remains

The cremated remains may be buried in a grave space in a family plot, at the foot of an occupied grave (with cemetery permission), or in a spot specially chosen by the family. A vault manufactured specifically for the cremation memorial is available for burial of the cremation memorial in the ground.

Placement in a Niche, Mausoleum, or Columbarium

Most cemeteries offer placement of the cremation memorial in a niche, mausoleum or columbarium, or a combination of all of them. They are generally above ground receptacles with brass, marble, or glass fronts. Your funeral service provider will be able to advise you as to what is available in your area.

Urn Garden

An urn garden is a special area in a cemetery designated for the burial of cremation memorials only. A marker is generally used to distinguish each plot.

Preparation of a "Remembering Place"

This is generally an area, selected and designated by the family, as the final place of remembrance after the cremated remains (also known as cremains) have been scattered. It provides a place for this and future generations to return to for honoring the deceased. It can take any form that the family desires.

Scattering Garden

This is an area in a cemetery where cremains may be scattered in a garden setting. Sometimes a large memorial is available where individual plaques may be placed in remembrance of those scattered there.

Cremation Urn May Be Taken Home

A family may elect to take the urn home and maintain it there. This is entirely a personal decision, and one that should be given careful consideration before a decision is made. Too often, a memorial urn can be lost or misplaced during a move, or sometimes even stolen or broken.

Scattering

The cremains may be scattered in a place of the family's choice, as long as it is in accordance with any Federal or State ordinances or laws. Your funeral service provider will be able to guide you about requirements in your area.

Other Options Available

To accommodate increasing requests from family members, a ceremonial casket is available to allow for visitation and traditional funeral without the purchase of the casket.

In addition, an increasing number of families are requesting the ceremonial casket at a memorial service.

Memorial services may be conducted with the cremation memorial present, and a picture of the deceased present. Many families are also including mementos, favorite possessions of the deceased, and other items that help make the service more customized and personalized. (I.E fishing pole, motorcycle, toy cars, miniature railroad, paintings, hats.)

A large number of families are requesting that their funeral service provider allow them to privately view the deceased prior to the cremation.

Service Options:

Night Service

Many families are finding that a service held at night with private interment the following day is increasing in popularity. This allows people who have difficulty leaving work to attend.

- Request the cost prior to making the decision, this can be expensive.
- Negotiate with the Funeral Service Provider to get a better cost

Private Service

A service held for members of the family and invited guests only. It is appropriate for the traditional funeral or memorial service.

- Request the cost prior to making the decision, this can be expensive.
- This is the most expensive of any service select.
- Get everything in writing prior to requesting the service.

Humanist Service

A non-religious service takes any form designated by the family and is conducted by a friend or relative.

Customized Services

Your Funeral Service Provider will assist you in arranging any service that meets your individual wishes and desires.

- Request the cost prior to making the decision, this can be expensive.

A Traditional Funeral with the Body Present and Cremation Following

A family who wishes to have a traditional funeral service and visitation with the body present may do so, and elect to have cremation follow the traditional funeral service.

Immediate Disposal with a Memorial Service

Families who wish to have the body cremated immediately may still select a memorial service. They may also elect to have the cremation memorial present, or not, as they so desire.

The cost of cremation typically ranges from $2,000 to $4,000 if arranged through a funeral home and from $1,500 to $3,000 if arranged directly through a crematory. Although the cost of cremation differs depending on locale, it's almost always substantially less than the cost of a full body burial -- which is one of the reasons cited for cremation's growing acceptance and popularity.

Cost of Cremation

In addition to the cost of the basic cremation service there are other charges added for related paperwork, merchandise, and services, including:

- Getting an original death certificate and copies.
- Obtaining a cremation permit releasing the body for cremation, usually issued by the state or county of residence vital records.
- Transporting the body from the place of death to the place of cremation.
- Disposition of the cremains.
- Purchasing or renting a casket or urn.

Although these incidental charges can add a few hundred to a few thousand dollars to the cost of cremation, the item that's potentially the priciest is a casket, which can range from $100 for a simple cardboard container to $5,500 for other style of wooden or metal caskets. Many people who choose cremation opt not to purchase a casket, but some prefer to have one during a funeral or memorial service at which the body will be present before cremation occurs. **(This is an area where you can save money)**

Options for Veterans

The U.S. Department of Veterans Affairs (VA) furnishes a partial reimbursement of eligible veterans' burial and funeral costs. When the cause of death is not service-related, the reimbursement is generally described as two payments: (1) burial and funeral expenses allowance, and (2) a plot interment allowance.

You may be entitled to a VA burial allowance if:

- You paid for a veteran's burial or funeral AND
- You have not been reimbursed by another government agency or some other source, such as the deceased veteran's employer AND
- The veteran was discharged under conditions other than dishonorable

In addition, at least one of the following conditions must be met:

- The veteran died because of a service-related disability.
- The veteran was getting VA pension or compensation at the time of death.
- The veteran was entitled to receive VA pension or compensation but decided not to reduce his/her military retirement or disability pay.
- The veteran died in a VA hospital or while in a nursing home under VA contract.

Service-related death:
The VA will pay an allowance toward burial expenses.

Non-service related death:
The VA will pay an allowance toward burial and funeral expenses, and a plot interment allowance. If the death happened while the veteran was in a VA hospital or under contracted nursing care, the cost of moving the deceased may be reimbursed.

Headstones and Markers
- The VA furnishes upon request, at no charge to the applicant, a Government headstone or marker to mark the unmarked grave of an eligible veteran in any cemetery around the world.

- Flat bronze, granite or marble markers and upright granite and marble headstones are available. The style chosen must be consistent with existing monuments at the place of burial. Niche markers are also available to mark columbaria used for inurnment of cremated remains.

Location Options:

Funeral Home Chapel, Chapel in a Cemetery, or a Church
A traditional funeral may be conducted in the funeral home chapel, a chapel in a cemetery, or the church of your choice. Your funeral service provider will help you with your choice.

Memorial Services Locations

A memorial service may be conducted in the funeral home chapel, a chapel in a cemetery, a church, at the home of the deceased, a relative or a friend, or any place you select.

Service at the Crematorium

A brief service may be held at the crematorium, with the body present, prior to cremation. Due to most space limitations, this is generally limited to family and close friends. (Witness of the placing body in crematory only)

Service at the Graveside

A memorial service may be held at the graveside, prior to interment or inurnment of the cremation memorial.

Any Location a Family Finds Meaningful and That Meets Their Needs and Wishes

Today's funeral services and cremation services are more customized and personalized than in the past, and may be conducted in a place of the family's choice. Your funeral service provider will be happy to assist you in arranging the service of your choice.

Cost Savings associated with the five (5) selections listed above.

- Review all cost related to the service selected above.
- Determine what fulfills your wishes prior to making any selection.
- Negotiate with the funeral service provider to get a better price on your selection.

REASONS TO PRE-PLAN YOUR FUNERAL

A death is always stressful to the survivors. They must cope with their grief, interrupt their normal routines to attend to the details of a visitation and funeral and begin adjusting to life without the person who died. In most cases, families also have the added burden of actually planning the funeral.

Pre-arranging makes sense. It is the process of making your funeral service plans and paying for those plans before your death. You can remove some of the emotional burden from your family by planning your funeral ahead of time. Pre-arranging a funeral ensures that your funeral will reflect your wishes and prevents grief stricken relatives from having to make difficult, last minute decisions.

Families who plan ahead realize the importance of this step and how much help it will be for everyone concerned when death becomes a reality. Most people find that pre-arranging gives them peace of mind because they have taken the initiative to help their families with these responsibilities and disturbing tasks.

A pre-need counselor can assist you in completing all the details of your pre-arranged funeral. Call the mortuary of your choice to receive a complete explanation of selections and prices.

By making your pre-arrangements today, you are also making sure that spiraling inflation will not jeopardize your family income or your wishes for your funeral service.

PRE-NEED FUNERAL PLANNING

No one likes to think about the end of life, but it is inevitable. When it comes, too often a family is left unprepared. They must not only deal with their grief, but also with the numerous details and costs of funeral arrangements.

Today's trend is toward sensible pre-planning of your funeral. Your thoughtfulness now can protect your family from the unexpected financial and emotional strain of their loss. Call your local mortuary to examine their funeral planning services. You can plan and finance your complete funeral service today before the need arises. The advantages make sense. Planning your own funeral:

- Makes your final wishes known.
- Means your family can be involved in making these difficult decisions.
- Relieves your loved ones of the financial responsibility of final costs.

Your pre-funded arrangements (called pre-need) allow your life insurance benefits to assist your survivors with living expenses for the future. Your funeral cost will not be taken from their income. Pre-funding a funeral offers you the advantage of paying for your funeral now, thus relieving your family of possible financial burden later.

There are two ways to pre-fund a funeral. The first is to enter into a trust fund agreement. Here, you deposit a specified amount of money (in a lump sum or monthly installments) into a fund that is managed by a trustee appointed by the funeral company. This fund is then used to pay for the funeral services and merchandise at the time of your death.

The second option is to purchase a specially designed insurance policy that provides benefits for funeral expenses. Any insurance company that offers life insurance will give you the option of using your life insurance benefit to pay for funeral expenses.

FINANCING YOUR PLAN

A good Funeral Service Provider will have a very simple plan, which could save you large sums of money by just spending a little time now.

If something happened to you today, would your family know what to do?

Would final arrangements be made exactly as you wish?

Funeral arrangements are one of the realities of life . . . and one of the most neglected areas in people's future planning. Studies show that families who have not pre-planned often spend more for the funeral services of a loved one.

An independent funeral planner will assist you in obtaining the best plan possible. Since these professionals are independent, they do not have a stake in the mortuary or the burial service you choose. The funeral plan you select will:

- Lock in your price no matter what happens to the cost of funerals in the future, you pay no more.
- Lock in the complete service of your choice (as elaborate or simple as you wish).
- Lock in your decisions to save your family difficult decisions at a time of sorrow.
- Lock in the price for peace of mind in knowing your family will be spared unforeseen expenses.

Many mortuaries have designed methods that allow you to plan and finance a complete funeral service today. They should guarantee a full service (as elaborate or simple as you wish) and help through the difficult planning process in advance.

You should be able to select from single or monthly payment terms and receive a written guarantee (called an irrevocable assignment) that ensures that no matter what happens to the costs of funerals in the future, your price will remain the same.

Take the time to call your local mortuary to learn more about the thoughtful advantages of pre-planning. Review of the plans can be done either at the funeral home or in the privacy of your own home with a trained counselor.

A pre-need counselor can assist you in completing all the details of pre-arrangement. You may choose any items that meet your needs.

Without cost or obligation, you should receive the facts about pre-need funeral planning. Call your provider for full details of the comprehensive funeral planning advice that they offer.

MEMORIAL PLAN

Most mortuaries are fully qualified and authorized to help you with a prepayment plan designed and approved specifically for funeral planning.

Without cost or obligation, they will explain exactly the way the program will work for you. They will review the many funeral services, merchandise options available, and other important details. Anyone can qualify.

Once you have made your decision, you tell them exactly what funeral service you wish. They will keep the information on file so there is no doubt about your expressed wishes and there will be no family disputes or involvement by others who may not know what you wanted.

Your loved ones will not need to ask: Did we do the right thing? Did we spend too much or too little? Is it what he or she wanted? Did we forget anything?

All of that is eliminated because it is in writing. If you choose to prepay, you may choose the payment plan that best suits your budget. If you should relocate, you do not have to cancel; your plan goes with you. Contact the new mortuary to ensure that they will accept the plan.

If you are one of those who have already taken advantage of a pre-arrangement plan and have everything prepared in advance, you are to be commended. When the death occurs, the survivor will simply call:

The mortuary where arrangements were made:

_____

_____

Should any important information change regarding your pre-arranged funeral plans, please contact the mortuary where you made the arrangements.

Location of your pre-arranged documents:

_____

FUNERAL INSTRUCTIONS

Name _____

Selected Funeral Services _____

Clergy/Rabbi Preference_____

Casket Selected/Preferred _____

Vault or Urn Selected/Preferred _____

Clothing Preference _____

Cemetery Name/Location _____

Receiving Funeral Home (if applicable) _____

Disposition Preference:

☐   Burial/Entombment   ☐   Donation
        Cremation   Shipment out of state

Funeral expense figures expressed are approximate and subject to change unless
protected by a pre-paid funeral agreement or an insurance policy.

_____

_____

_____

_____

Pre-need # (if applicable) _____

Special instructions:

_____

_____

_____

_____

The above information specifies my wishes at the time of my death. It is intended to assist those
handling my personal affairs. I have expressed my preference on certain subjects that, unless
changed by unexpected circumstances, I hereby desire and request. My signature certifies that
the information herein is correct.

Witness (Counselor) _____

Signature_____

Date of Arrangements _____

Printed Name _____

Next Time
By Gary M. Thomas

When next you see her
she'll be smiling again
telling you stories
remembering when.
When next you see her
a smile on her face
you'll remember the first day
and all of her grace.
When next you see her
she'll be out of her pain,
welcoming you and
smiling again
and that special smile
that lights up your heart
will shine like a
candle out of the dark
when next you see her,
again.

Once you have made your choices for your memorialization ceremony, it is vital that you plan your Estate distribution according to your wishes.

WILLS

One of the first steps to take in organizing your Estate for your heirs is to prepare a *Will*. A *Will* is a legal, binding document that instructs the State and your family of your wishes for your personal assets. A *Will* is a document you create to control who gets your property, who will be the guardian of your children, and who will manage your estate upon your death.

The importance of a *Will* cannot be overstated. "A *Will* is possibly the most important legal document the average person will ever sign. Yet, over 70% of American adults do not have a *Will*. Not enough time, cannot afford an attorney, too busy to think about it - - are all common reasons why people do not prepare wills. In addition, none of us like to consider our own mortality, which is why so many families are caught unprepared." (LegalZoom.com)

There are multiple options for completing a *Will*. The first is to see an attorney. If you are assigning guardianship for minor children, you MUST see an attorney. The second option is to purchase a "*Will*" form from a local Office Supply Store or to visit the Web and type in "Will" for your search and you will have many options from which to choose.

Ensure that all property is included in your *Will*. Do not assume that former documents will cover existing property. In some instances, joint ownership of property may not be a good substitute for a carefully drafted *Will*. As a result of a common accident, both you and your spouse may die before the survivor has had an opportunity to execute a proper *Will*. In this case, your property will pass according to state law.

Personal Representative: - Executor of Your *Will* -

If you choose to use an attorney, be prepared to provide your attorney with the names and addresses of the people with whom you want to share your Estate. You will also need to decide who will act as your Personal Representative (also called the Executor of your *Will*). Your Personal Representative will often be your spouse, one or several of your children, or a close family member – it must be someone you trust.

After death, it is the responsibility of the Personal Representative to contact an attorney and begin Estate proceedings including the filing of the current *Will* with the probate court. A *Will* is valid when it has been fully executed with witnesses.

A VALID WILL *SHOULD* MUST BE FILED WITH THE COURT WITHIN TEN (10) DAYS FROM THE DATE OF DEATH,

Your Personal Representative will petition the probate court for authority to act as your Personal Representative (or executor). He/she will have the responsibility of collecting all assets of your estate, paying debts and legal obligations, having the assets appraised, and distributing your estate to the people designated in your Will.

Your Personal Representative is entitled to a fee for administering your Estate. This fee depends upon the responsibilities placed upon him/her to manage your estate. Reasonable fees for payment include: gathering assets, paying off debts, appraising assets, etc. Your Personal Representative has the option to waive these fees.

No Will on File

If you die without a Will, state law and the courts determine who will administer your estate, handle financial matters, and act as guardian for your minor children. With a Will, you choose. If no Will exists, your legal heirs will be determined in accordance with state law.

Should an individual die without having a current valid Will, it is the responsibility of the heirs to engage an attorney. Their attorney will properly open the Estate and file it with the Court's Probate Division. Probate is the process of concluding your affairs, accumulating your assets, paying your debts, and distributing your assets to the heirs as determined by the state laws.

State Law

The law is very exacting in its requirements with respect to the publication, signing and witnessing of Wills. It is recommended that a competent attorney handle this matter.

Homemade Wills often do not stand up in court. However, this is a valid option if you do not own many personal assets and do not have minor children that need guardianship. Store bought and online legal documentation services are not a law firm, do not represent you and are not a substitute for the advice of an attorney. These services help you represent yourself in your own legal matters. If you are involved in litigation or have complex legal issues, hire an attorney.

Review of Will

You should review your Will every few years to be sure that it reflects your current intentions and desires. State laws vary as to formal requirements and as to the rights of children and grandchildren born after a Will was executed. Update your Will to include all new children or grandchildren that have been born but are not yet included in the last version of your Will. You can change your Will by adding a Codicil to your existing Will or by revoking the old Will and having a new one prepared.

If you have a valid Will that was prepared in another state, have a local attorney review it to ensure that it meets the requirements of the State's Statutes and to determine whether it will have an adverse effect on the distribution of your property. In most cases, it is advisable to draft a new Will in your state, if only to avoid the expense of locating out-of-state witnesses.

When you realize how much is at stake...the well-being of your entire family and the protection of your property... you will find that the attorney's fee for drafting your Will and planning your estate is a worthwhile investment.

LIVING WILL

A Living Will is a document that instructs doctors and your loved one's of your wishes and desires regarding whether or not your life is prolonged by artificial means. You may also express your wishes regarding medical treatment to prolong your life under certain circumstances. It also provides a provision for an anatomical gift donation.

An attorney may draft this for you, you may pick up a form from your doctor before a major surgery, or you can find this form in many local Office Supply Stores or in an online search (type in living will).

A Living Will must be witnessed. One of the witnesses must not be a spouse or blood relative of the Declarant. An example of a Living Will is below. Complete this form while you are in good health and of sound mind.

SAMPLE LIVING WILL

Declaration made this _____ day of_____ 20____

I, _____willfully and voluntarily make known my desire that my dying shall not be artificially prolonged under the circumstances set forth below, and do hereby declare:

If at any time I should have a terminal condition and my attending physician has determined that there can be no recovery from such condition and my death is eminent, where the application of life-prolonging procedures would serve only to artificially prolong the dying process. I direct that such procedures be withdrawn or withheld, and that I be permitted to die naturally with only the administration of medication or the performance of any medical procedure deemed necessary to provide me with comfort care or to alleviate pain.

In addition, whether or not my death is imminent. I direct that, if I have a terminal condition or am irreversibly unconscious, nutrition and hydration (food and water) not be provided by tubing or intravenously.

In the absence of my ability to give directions regarding the use of such life prolonging procedures, it is my intention that this declaration shall be honored by my family and physician as the final expression of my legal right to refuse medical or surgical treatment and accept the consequences for such refusal.

Should I become comatose, incompetent, or otherwise mentally or physically incapable of communication, I authorize:

_____

(Name. address and telephone)
to make treatment decisions on my behalf in accordance with my Living Will Declaration. If my designated representative is not readily available, my directions in this Declaration should be carried out without the concurrence of the representative.

If I have been diagnosed as pregnant and my physician knows that diagnosis, this Declaration shall have no force or effect during the course of my pregnancy.

I understand the full import of this Declaration and I am emotionally and mentally competent to make this Declaration.

Signature

_____

The Declarant is known to me and I believe him/her to be of sound mind.

Witness _____ Date _____
Witness _____ Date _____

Live Your Life Today
By
Gary M. Thomas

Watching the mountains change color
as dawn turns into day
gives new meaning to the saying
live your life today.
Tomorrows a distant wish list
that can be taken away
don't build a dream house on it
live your life today.
Don't look into the future
it can go various ways
exist in the moment's fullness
live your life today.
When in your final moments,
before you fade away
look back in relief,
without sorrow or grief
cause you lived your life today.

Once you have planned your Estate, it is important to review and outline the benefits that loved ones should expect at the time of your death.

LIFE INSURANCE BENEFITS

Generally, death benefits paid to a Named beneficiary are not taxable or included in the total of the deceased's estate. Insurance proceeds left to the estate, or with no surviving beneficiaries, must be filed in the probate proceedings.

Proceeds from the policy may be paid to the beneficiary in different ways. Proper advice can help resolve investment questions. Life insurance benefits are for the surviving family. A pre-funded funeral plan can secure these funds for day-to-day expenses that the survivors must meet.

As part of their services, some mortuaries will assist you in claiming the life insurance benefits of the insured deceased. They maintain a complete file of the major companies' claims forms. They may also assist in changing other policies where the stated beneficiary is the deceased.

Insurance Benefits may be available from:
- Life insurance
- Group insurance (i.e., place of employment)
- Fraternal and Civic organizations
- Credit card insurance, available through major credit card companies
- Credit life insurance (mortgages, vehicles, personal loans)
- Car insurance, Personal Injury Protection (PIP)/No Fault
- Home Owners Policy (under certain applications)
- Government life insurance
- Veterans life insurance

If you have concerns regarding policies that may be in force, but are not available, contact:

The American Council of Life Insurance
Information and Reference Service
1001 Penn Avenue NW.
Washington D.C. 02004

This service assists in locating lost or unattainable policies. Contact the local agent who may have more detailed information regarding other policies the insured may have with the company.

Necessary Documents for claiming Benefits:

1. One certified death certificate for each insurance company.
2. Properly completed claim form signed by beneficiary.
3. If the beneficiary is deceased, a certified death certificate of that person should accompany the claim.
4. Change of Beneficiary endorsement.
5. A copy of the insurance policy.
6. Proof of marriage/marriage license.
7. Proof of payment of funeral expense, when all beneficiaries are deceased and proceeds go to the estate.

Death Benefits may be assigned to pay funeral expenses.

Insurance Company	Phone #	Face Amount	Policy #	Beneficiary

MEDICAL INSURANCE

A surviving spouse should contact the medical insurance company as soon as possible and review his or her own coverage.

If a refund of premiums is in order for the deceased, a certified death certificate will be needed to claim the refund.

If premiums are automatically withdrawn from a bank account, notify the insurance company first and then take a death certificate to the bank to stop payment to the insurance company.

Use the following page to outline major medical information.

MEDICAL EMERGENCY CARD INFORMATION

Name_____

Address _____

City, State, Zip_____

Do you have a Living Will? _____ Yes _____ No

What is your blood type? _____

Are you allergic to medications? _____ Yes _____ No
If so, what are they?

_____

_____

Are you currently taking medications? _____ Yes _____No
If so, what are they?

_____

_____

Do you wear contact lenses/glasses? _____Yes _____ No
Do you have any special devices? (i.e. pacemaker, etc) ____Yes ____No
If so, what are they?

_____

_____

My doctor is:

Name_____

Address _____

City, State, Zip_____

Phone_____

SOCIAL SECURITY BENEFITS

It is a good idea to check your Social Security record every three years to make sure that earnings are being correctly reported to your record.

Your funeral director sends the "Statement of Death by Funeral Director" (form 721) to the local social security office, but you must contact the social security office to apply for any benefits.

The Social Security Administration will make a lump sum payment when an eligible person dies. This payment can only be made if there is an eligible surviving widow, widower, entitled child or to certain members of the worker's family.

Benefits are available to the following:

1. Unmarried children under 18 (or under 19 if a full-time high school student).
2. Unmarried son or daughter 18 or over who was severely disabled before 22 and who continues to be disabled.
3. Widow or widower 60 or older.
4. Widow or widower, or surviving divorced mother or father if caring for worker's child under 18 (or disabled) who is getting a benefit based on the earnings of the deceased worker.
5. Widow or widower 50 or older who becomes disabled not later than 7 years after the workers death, or within 7 years after mothers or father's benefits end.
6. Dependent parents 62 years old or older.
7. Benefits are payable to a divorced spouse at 62 or over, a surviving divorced spouse at 60 or to a disabled surviving divorced spouse 50 or older if the marriage was of 10 years or more.
8. Under certain conditions, children may be eligible for Social Security benefits based on a grandparent's earnings.

A divorced spouse who has been divorced at least 2 years, and has been married for at least 10 years (to the deceased) can receive benefits at 62 whether or not his or her former spouse receives benefits. The former spouse must be eligible for Social Security benefits regardless of whether he or she has retired. Survivors can get benefits in most cases if the marriage was at least 9 months long.

The amount of income will be determined by the Social Security Administration based on:

(1) Number of working quarters.
(2) Amount paid into Social Security.

Contacting Your Local Social Security Office

To facilitate receiving Social Security benefits, you will need the following when you contact your Social Security Office:

1. Deceased Social Security Number
2. Children's Birth Certificates (for dependent children under 18)
3. W2 forms of deceased, if worked within the last two years prior to death
4. Proof of widow(er)'s age if 62 years or older
5. Certified Copy of Death Certificate
6. Military discharge papers for additional benefits

An application for the lump sum death payments usually must be made within two years after the worker's death. Do not delay applying because you do not have all the proof of information. The customer service representatives in the Social Security Office will inform you of the proof of information that can be used when you apply. The toll free phone number for the Social Security Administration is 1-800-772-1213.

Record your information here:

Social Security Number of (name)   Social Security Number

_____   _____

_____   _____

Address of Nearest Social Security Office:

_____

_____

Social Security Benefits Mailed to the Deceased

Benefits received prior to the date of death are earned and may be kept. Any benefits received for the month following the date of death and any subsequent months **must be returned.**

Social Security Benefits Direct Deposited

If monthly benefits are directly deposited into a bank account, contact your social security office to verify when payments will be received. Time to process benefits may vary, but benefits payable are retroactive from the month of application.

Social Security Earning Capacity

Earning capacity is the dollar amount you are allowed to earn that will not affect the benefits you receive. Contact your local Social Security office to verify the current amount you are permitted to earn based on your present age. Benefits will be reduced $1.00 for every $3.00 earned between the ages of 59 and 65.

Taxable income should be determined and filed by a qualified tax person and submitted with your usual income tax at year-end.

VETERANS' BURIAL BENEFITS

Various veteran's benefits may be available to the survivors of an eligible deceased veteran. They consist of burial allowance and monthly survivor benefits.

Burial Flags

Most veterans are eligible for a burial flag. Reservists entitled to retired pay are also eligible to receive a burial flag.

Ensure that you carefully file for all burial allowances, flags and markers for which the deceased veteran may be eligible.

Necessary Documentation for Veteran Benefits

To facilitate receiving veteran benefits, you will need the following when you contact the Veterans Administration Office:

1. Copy of Veterans military discharge or Proof of the veteran's military service (DD 214)
2. Service Serial Number
3. Original or certified copy of Marriage License (if applicable)
4. If there were previous marriages on either side, original or certified copy of divorce decree or certified death certificate
5. Original or certified copy of Children's Birth Certificate of children under 18, older if attending school, or helpless before 18th birthday
6. Certified Copy of the Death Certificate
7. VA claim number, if one has been issued
8. VA insurance policy or number
9. Social Security numbers of husband, widow, children and original or current award letter, statement of other pension, annuity, etc.
10. Funeral and/or cemetery property bills (Only paid bills accepted)

All survivor benefits should be applied for through your local Veteran's Service Office as soon as possible after death. Burial benefits may be applied for up to two (2) years following the death of an eligible veteran.

Benefits have been extended to those who served in the Merchant Marines during wartime and were honorably discharged. To apply, contact the local V.A. office or State office.

All benefits received in the name of the deceased veteran following the death **MUST BE RETURNED** to the local Veterans Service Office. Proper evaluation of eligibility for funds will be determined on behalf of the survivors. CONTACT YOUR LOCAL OFFICE FOR APPLICATION.

The Toll Free Phone Number for the Veterans' Administration is 1-800-827-1000.

Discharge and other veteran's documents are located at:

_____

Benefits expected include:

_____

CIVIL SERVICE FEDERAL EMPLOYEE BENEFITS

The exact type of benefits and the amount received will depend on each individual case. Benefits could include an adjustment of health insurance coverage from "self and family" to "self only", provided the survivor has been previously covered. If the deceased person provided for the survivor's coverage, there is also a Survivor annuity. Any annuity benefits that have not been paid will be included in the benefits paid to the eligible survivor.

An application for survivor's benefits must be completed before the Employee Service and Record Center can authorize any payments of possible benefits. This application can be obtained from:

Office of Personnel Management
Employee Services and Records Center
Boyers, PA 16017
412-794-8442

The letter of notification should include:

1. The full name of the deceased
2. Date of birth of the deceased
3. Civil Service Account (CSA) number
4. Name, address and relationship of person who desires to obtain survivor's benefits

Civil Service Benefits

My CSA claim number is: _____

The Location of All Federal Employee Documents:

_____

_____

Benefits expected:

_____

_____

RAILROAD RETIREMENT BENEFITS

Currently, an employee is considered insured under the Railroad Retirement Benefits Program if he/she has at least ten (10) years of service and/or is connected with the Railroad at time of retirement.

An employee is considered Uninsured if he/she has less than ten (10) years of employment and has served in connection with the Railroad prior to retirement.

Benefits not payable under Railroad Retirement will be transferred to the Social Security Administration. Only one fund is required to make payments. Lump-Sum Death Benefits (sometimes called Residual Lump-Sum Payments) are assignable to the funeral services.

Benefits Available

Lump-Sum Death Payment (Residual Lump-Sum Payment) - insured status is not required. This is a fund for pre-1975 Railroad Retirement taxes, plus an allowance in lieu of interest. Form G-126 for residual benefits based on service under the Railroad Retirement Act is filed with the local board.

Annuities - are payable to widows/widowers, unmarried children under the age of 19 (attending high school or vocational school), or disabled children of any age who become disabled before age 22. Under certain cases, survivor annuity benefits may be payable to parents, remarried widow(ers), or surviving divorced spouses.

Address inquires to:
The United States Railroad Retirement Board
501 East Polk Street Room 100
Tampa, Florida 33602
Phone (813) 228-2695

To apply for Railroad Retirement benefits, mail a certified Death Certificate to the above address. Include a cover letter stating any previous contact you have made, the representative you spoke to and the benefits you expect. Representatives will handle all paperwork. Make sure to take the representative's name to follow up on your benefits.

Railroad Service Number is _____

Deceased Social Security number is _____

The Location of All Railroad Employee Documents:

_____

_____

_____

Benefits expected:

_____

_____

_____

Customer Service representative:

_____

Now that your Estate is planned and the benefits that your survivors should expect are outlined, it is time to finalize your financial business.

Some items to review include your personal income taxes, credit cards, vehicle titles, safe deposit box, additional insurance (auto, home, disability etc.) and any other pertinent financial information (such as current investments).

PERSONAL INCOME TAX

Under Federal Law, any earned personal income must be reported to the Internal Revenue Service. All individuals who meet the criteria for annual reporting of personal income must file a return the year following a death.

A surviving spouse may file a joint return in the year of a death. In addition, for two years following a death, a widowed individual (with at least one dependent child) may file at joint return rates provided a remarriage does not occur before the end of the taxable year. The widowed parent may file as head of household provided he/she remains unmarried after the two-year period.

Those individuals who are widowed before the deceased spouse has received any pension benefits may be entitled to a special income tax death benefit exclusion. It is important to seek advice from your tax consultant regarding your pension or annuity income when you are filing your tax return.

Surviving Spouse Filing an Estimated Quarterly Tax Return
The surviving spouse must continue to file remaining estimated quarterly tax returns. A photocopy of the death certificate should accompany the return stating the name of the deceased spouse, while indicating the surviving spouse's name and social security number.

Single Individual
Upon death, an individual who meets the requirements for filing personal income tax transfers this responsibility to the named personal representative. All payments due or refunds payable by the Internal Revenue Service will he applied to the deceased's estate.

Tax Requirements During the Open Estate Period
While a person's estate is being settled, the spouse or personal representative filing the personal income tax return may be required to file a Fiduciary Income Tax Form #1041. This form is used for the interim period when an estate is held open into the following taxable year.

Your professional tax consultant will assist you in completing all the necessary documents for the Internal Revenue Service. The following items should be available:

- Previous years tax return

- Form W-2 for current year earnings
- Form W-2P for current earning from pension, stocks, dividends, capital gains, and all other forms of miscellaneous income
- Form 1099, interest earning report from bank, lending institute, etc.

To ensure proper income and deductions have been reported, keep all pertinent current tax information placed in one location.

The location of my current tax papers:

_____

_____

Contact a tax consultant with any question you have.

CREDIT CARD TRANSACTIONS

Credit card transactions and proper transfer of account holder's name are very important following a death. To secure and maintain good credit the Personal Representative must notify the individual credit card company in writing of the cardholder's death. Include the following information in the letter to the credit card companies:

1. A statement informing the company of the death of the cardholder.
2. An inquiry to the open balance amount.
3. The name and address of the Personal Representative of the deceased.
4. Also include a statement inquiring whether or not the account is covered by credit life insurance.

If the account was a joint account, the joint account holder may retain the card issued in their own name, all others must be returned. Inform the credit card company that the account will now be changed to an individual account. Each credit card company will determine the liability of the account.

A complete and current list of all credit cards should be maintained with your important documents such as your Will. You may also keep the information in this book.

Company	Phone Number	Name on the Account	Card Number	Exp Date

TITLE TRANSFER REQUIREMENTS

All vehicles and vessels must be listed in the total asset tabulation and tax evaluation. Vehicles and vessels include:

- Cars/trucks/vans
- Mobile homes
- Motorcycles or mopeds
- Recreation vehicles (campers, motor homes)
- Vessels/boats (separate classification)

All forms and title transfers can be done at a local tag (DMV) agency with the county where your vehicles are registered.

Depending on how the title is registered (joint ownership, or sole ownership), the following documents may be necessary:

- Title of vehicle
- Name and location of lien holder to title
- Certified death certificate for each vehicle
- Current registration
- Certified copy of Will stating direct beneficiary if available
- Letter of Administration and Personal Representative appointed
- Odometer reading

Vehicles registered out-of-state must be registered in state before transfer of ownership can occur.

Classification of Title Transfers of Vehicles & Documents Required

The following outlines the type of titles that vehicles may be registered under and the documentation needed to transfer title:

Joint Ownership:
1. Certified death certificate per vehicle
2. Title of vehicle
3. Photo identification
4. Current registration

Sole Ownership:
1. Certified death certificate
2. Title of vehicle

Administration of Estate (No spouse - Heirs are required to have):
1. Letter of Administration
2. Title of vehicle
3. Certified death certificate

If additional forms are required they can be obtained at your local tag (DMV) agency.

Classification for Boat Title Transfer
The following outlines the type of titles that boats may be registered under and the documentation needed to transfer title:

Surviving Spouse (or Heirs):
1. Title - if no title is available, an affidavit stating the reason must be signed and notarized.
2. Certified death certificate.
3. Certified copy of current Will or Letter of Administration if estate is probated.

Applicant (Not Spouse or Heir), Wanting to Assume Ownership:
1. Form #10T24 completed by spouse or heirs.
2. Form #1 (on reverse side of title) signed and notarized.
3. Certified death certificate.
4. Certified copy of current Will or Letter of Administration if estate is probated.

Joint or Co-Ownership:
1. Form #10T24 completed by spouse or heirs.
2. Certified death certificate.

The location of my vehicle titles:

_____

_____

SAFE DEPOSIT BOX

It is important to keep records of your safe deposit box location and the contents of the box because the contents of safe deposit box must be reported to your attorney for asset tabulation. In most cases, safe deposit boxes are not sealed at the time of death.

A box with Sole Ownership (**no beneficiary),** requires the following for asset retrieval:

- Certified death certificate
- Letter of Administration issued by the bank
- Bank official and administrator (when possible) to retrieve the contents.

A box with multiple owner(s) will allow the surviving owner(s) to retrieve contents for asset tabulation. Your attorney can also collect these items for you.

My safe deposit box is located at:

_____

_____

The key to this box is located at:

_____

Other Financial Information

Review any additional financial information that may be pertinent to your situation. Some items to review may include additional insurance such as auto and homeowners insurance.

Take this time to review your current investments as well. Make any changes or adjustments you see fit.

The location of my important financial information:

_____

_____

_____

_____

Many additional forms are included at the back of this book to assist you in outlining the pertinent information that your survivors will need.

Completing the actions listed in this book and providing it to your heirs is one of the most important final steps you can take in ensuring your needs are met and their questions are answered.

Life
By Gary M. Thomas

Life is like a river.

It has a beginning, journey
and an ending.

We all have to start somewhere
which is our birth.

Our journey is a growing process
such as the journey of the river.

The end is death,
such as the river journey ends.

To meet another body of water.

Our journey is meeting God

VITAL STATISTICS

Full Name _____

Address _____

City, State, Zip _____

Phone _____

Length of Residence _____

Former Residence Address _____

City, State, Zip _____

Birth Place _____

Birth Date _____ U.S. Citizen _____

Schooling 1 2 3 4 5 6 7 8 9 10 11 12   College 1 2 3 4 5 6 7+

Father's Name _____

Mother's Maiden Name _____

_____ Never Married   _____ Divorced   _____ Spouse (Maiden Name)

Social Security Number _____

Church Affiliation

Address _____

City, State, Zip _____

Phone _____

Clubs, Organizations, Memberships

_____

_____

_____

_____

Place of Employment

Address _____

City, State, Zip _____

Type of Business/Industry _____

How Long? _____

Occupation _____

Retired? Y/N _____

Veteran of Service

_____ Yes _____ No

Serial Number _____

War

_____

_____

Time of Service

_____

_____

Branch & Rank

_____

_____

SURVIVORS TO NOTIFY AT THE TIME OF DEATH

Relationship	In Will? Y/N	Name	Address	Phone

\# of Grandchildren_____

\# of Great Grandchildren _____

Personal Representative

Name_____

Address _____

City, State, Zip_____

Phone_____

PROFESSIONAL ADVISORS

Accountant

Name _____

Address _____

City, State, Zip _____

Phone _____

Attorney

Name _____

Address _____

City, State, Zip _____

Phone _____

Banker

Name _____

Address _____

City, State, Zip _____

Phone _____

Clergy/Rabbi

Name _____

Address _____

City, State, Zip _____

Phone _____

Insurance Agent

Type *(life, medical, auto, home)* _____

Name _____

Address _____

City, State, Zip _____

Phone _____

Insurance Agent

Type *(life, medical, auto, home)* _____

Name _____

Address _____

City, State, Zip _____

Phone _____

Insurance Agent

Type (*life, medical, auto, home*) _____

Name _____

Address _____

City, State, Zip _____

Phone _____

Realtor

Name _____

Address _____

City, State, Zip _____

Phone _____

Stockbroker

Name _____

Address _____

City, State, Zip _____

Phone _____

Advisor

Name _____

Address _____

City, State, Zip _____

Phone _____

Gary M. Thomas, MBA, CFSP, CMSP. Gary graduated from Columbia College with a Bachelor Degree in Business Administration and earned his Master's Degree from the University of Phoenix. Gary has been involved in all aspects of the mortuary and funeral business including funeral home ownership and management. His experience includes both family and corporate owned funeral homes and cemeteries.

Currently, Gary is Assistant Manager for Fairmount Mortuary. He is Vice President of the Colorado Funeral Directors Association for 2010-2012.

He has over 15 years of experience with a Fortune 500 company in management and marketing. Gary has been teaching at numerous colleges in the Denver area the past twelve years, winning multiple awards as the 'Outstanding Instructor'. Gary has also published magazine articles on the funeral service business.

Printed in the United States
By Bookmasters